Y: Christian Millennial Manifesto © 2017 by Joshua Best

Contact the author:
www.joshuabestcreative.com | twitter: @joshuabest
joshuabestcreative@gmail.com | instagram: joshuadavidbest

Contact the publisher:
Unprecedented Press LLC - 495 Sleepy Hollow Ln, Holland, MI 49423
www.unprecedentedpress.com | info@unprecedentedpress.com
twitter: @UnprecdntdPress | instagram: unprecedentedpress

ISBN-10:0-9861931-8-6
ISBN-13:978-0-9861931-8-7

Printed in the United States of America
Ingram Printing & Distribution, 2017
Edited by Rose White

First Edition

Unprecedented Press

Y

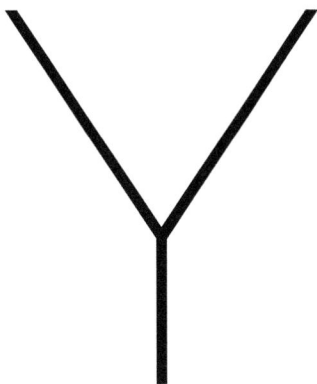

CHRISTIAN MILLENNIAL MANIFESTO

Joshua Best

FOREWORD BY
Joshua Luke Smith

Un
Pɹ

TABLE OF CONTENTS

To my parents and my children,
may I be a faithful bridge,
a son that brings honor,
and a generous father.

ACKNOWLEDGEMENTS

I want to thank the following people for lending me their wisdom through interviews and emails. Your words live verbatim in a few short quotes in this book and the companion workbook, but your advice will remain in my heart forever.

Eleanor Best	Dave Roberts
Mary Jay	Carol Roberts
Stephen Best	Jim Soper
Cindy Best	Diane Soper
Mike Dugan	Bob Lemon
Jeff Johnson	

I'd like to thank Andrew & Angela Hughes for providing me a place to grow and serve the Lord at The Point Church. I will never forget how you entrusted April and I with the young adults. The lessons we learned under your watchful eyes will bear fruit for years to come.

Of course, I need to thank my wife April for her support, patience, and endless grace throughout this process.

Lastly, I'd like to thank Rose White for editing the book. Thanks for lending me your brain.

FOREWORD
by Joshua Luke Smith

The first time I met Josh, I was in a crowded room full of people I didn't know. I'd been in the U.S. for only a few days, still jet lagged. But I was buzzing from consuming copious amounts of coffee, which is served in what seemed like vats compared to the microscopic servings I'm used to in England. I was in America to share at a conference, meet with a record label, and catch up with old friends. But since I had arrived in Grand Rapids, I had taken on a new and more purpose-driven mission – to meet Josh. It seemed like everyone I met since stepping off the plane had eagerly told me, "Oh, you have to meet Josh." So, when we shook hands in that crowded room full of strangers, I knew it would be good.

In 2011, my wife and I started a record label called Orphan No More, but it's really more than that. It's our family. It's our community. It's our expression of something bigger than ourselves. And it's our desire to stand upon a soapbox and declare a simple message: one that our generation is groaning to hear and know in their innermost being – you are not an orphan. You are not alone, the story isn't over, and you still have a message to share and a song that must be sung.

The promise that Jesus made to his followers, as they sat together over broken bread and glasses of red wine the evening before the world would change forever, was that he would not leave them as they were. He wouldn't leave them as those who are looking for love, validation, recognition and hope in all the wrong places, but he would reveal to them his Father, a God in pursuit of man, a God they can't outrun.

I believe this Millennial generation, of which I am apart, sits at the table, longing to hear those words. We're longing to find out who we truly are, yearning to know there's more, desperate to get a glimpse of something bigger than ourselves. We have been told we are self-absorbed, idealistic, and though conscious of the environment, more wasteful than any generation before us. We have been told we are unpatriotic, greedy, immoral, and the least hardworking generation to date. We know what we like flat whites, vintage clothes, vintage cameras, and vintage, well, everything. We have scrolled through our twenties and now we are scrolling through our thirties on a device that can tell us everything, except the one question even Siri can't answer:

Who are we?

In an age of information we seem to be both uninformed and ill-informed, but there is nothing we have been so greatly deceived about than our identity. Like pilgrims in a desert, we await the voice of those crying out in the wilderness, leading us into the fullness of our true selves, telling us our new name. When God renamed Abram to Abraham, it was both a prophetic declaration of who he would become and a moment of healing, binding the wounds of who he had been.

Abraham took matters into his own hands. He benched God in the belief that he could, in his independence, bypass the process and get straight to the product. He slept with a servant that bore him a son, but it was not the son God had promised. That act brought on some 13 years of silence between him and God, which was broken by this moment where God gives him a new name. Abraham's first name meant "honored father," but his second name meant "father of a multitude." For Abraham, this would not be a name to live up to, but a name to live down. Every time it was called, he would shudder under the shame of what he felt he could never be – how hollow the promise seemed and how far he felt from it. But when God speaks, he does only in truth and sometimes the truth hurts. Why? Because we build houses of comfort with walls made out of fear. And when He speaks, His truth shatters the windows like a wind. It rips up the floorboards and exposes every crack and piece of rotten timber in this beaten shack we call home.

We cry out, "God, I live here! What are you doing?" And He cries back, "I'm loving you. I'll never compromise my Word for the sake of your comfort."

I believe this book has the power to speak – like God did to Abraham that day – and rename a generation with it's true name as both a prophetic declaration and a process of healing. We are not what has been said about us, nor defined by our failings. This is not how the story ends. In this book, Josh reveals that God is a potter, a master craftsman, an artisan who knows what he is forming. No matter where you are, no matter what you've done, he will never redesign the blueprint plans that will reveal what you will become.

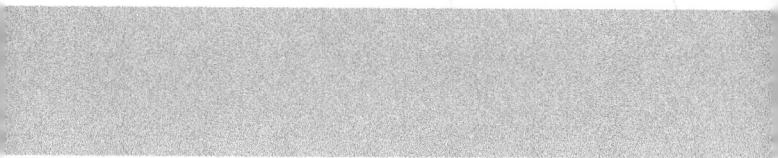

INTRODUCTION

'm a Millennial. I was born in 1984 – the year George Orwell warned us about, and the year Steve Jobs introduced the Macintosh. I was about eleven years old when everything changed: tapes switched to CDs, cell phones became mainstream, and computers were magically connected to the internet. I was sixteen when we entered the new millennium, and I graduated from college in 2008. I'm telling you this to gain your trust. Not as a parent, teacher, or social scientist. No, I'm writing to you as a peer.

Unfortunately, that means I'm not exempt from subjectivity, and I'm sure that as you read this book, my bias will become evident. You will sense my own Millennial thought process. I tried my best not to sing the praises of my generation, but to focus on the possibilities that lie in front of us if we act according to our full potential. If, as a Millennial, you think I'm coming off too critical – just remember, I'm one of you.

I'm also a pastor. I lead a church called The Point Holland with people from every generation, but I also oversee the young adult ministry across a few campuses along with a great team of leaders. The ministry is called The Point Exchange and through it, I've been gathering, teaching and provoking young adults for over seven years. That's my resume. Hopefully, it tells you I'm qualified to write on this topic. What it can't tell you is that I'm deeply passionate about our generation, so I will try my best to convey that passion in the words I write.

Why Y? Good question. Hang on as I explain.

SOLID WHITE LINES

Have you ever been driving on a major, multi-lane highway and missed your exit? When it happens, you get that panicked feeling, and you wonder if there's still time to change lanes. Sometimes, when I'm in that situation, I'll find myself overcome by an immediate and urgent sense of boldness, which causes me to cross the solid white lines and narrowly avoid the side rails or the barrels full of water. At other times, I'm not so bold or it's too late and the part of my brain that analyzes space and time makes a judgment call – and, presumably, saves my life.

A couple years ago, I was working for an advertising agency that required me drive to Chicago once a month. I live in West Michigan, so the drive was not too far – about three hours one way. Since it was within a reasonable driving distance, I would rent a car the night before, drive there early in the morning, spend the day with the team, and drive home at night. It was a long day, but I love traveling so it didn't bother me. On one particular trip, it was dark when I left downtown Chicago. I had a colleague with me in the rental car, and I needed to get onto the highway from South Lake Shore Drive. Instead of preparing the GPS on our phones before leaving, we fumbled around and tried to find directions while driving. By the time we identified the proper route, we had almost missed our onramp. I was driving, and I had one of the moments I described to you. My gut took over. I saw the solid white lines, so I looked ahead and gauged the distance between us and the impending hazard. I looked in my blindspot, and the lane on the other side of the white lines looked empty. So, I went for it.

In traffic terminology, there's a term for the land, which is contained by those solid white lines and ultimately separates a ramp from the main road. It's called a gore. It usually begins as a curb and turns into a more prominent structure like a barrier wall. It's often adorned with hazard signs or reflectors. When I made the decision in my gut to cross the solid white lines, I hadn't realized there was a curb in between them. When I swerved right to change lanes, we were shocked by the bump we experienced. I didn't immediately know what we'd hit, so I just kept going. A couple thuds later, we were in the lane I was aiming for. As it turns out, we went directly over the gore. It was a four-foot wide section of curb that I drove over – in a compact car nonetheless. This scenario is similar to the one we are in today as Christian Millennials. Let me explain.

When I was in college, we studied the characteristics of each generation. They were specific to the Western world and focused on the ones that are still alive today. It was 2005. At that time, scholars were still using the term Generation Y to describe us. The information they gave us made me feel proud to be in Gen Y. Their description painted a picture of young people who were community-minded, responsible, creative, and confident. Skip forward ten years or so, and the rhetoric takes a detour. Now, workplaces are struggling to integrate Millennials into the workforce, and society keeps telling us we're entitled, narcissistic and unfocused. Paul Taylor and the Pew Research Center described this shift in social perception in the book entitled *The Next America*. In the book, they discuss journalists and authors who painted a generous portrait of Millennials when it was all about *we*. Years later, they claim, articles about Millennials became all about *me*.

The way we're perceived by other generations changed at some point. Did we do something to sabotage their first impressions of us, or did they finally discover who we really are? In my opinion, we didn't change – and that's the issue. Instead of adjusting properly into adulthood and staying on track, we've continued in the same direction, which now means we're off course. It's as if we looked down at our phones for a second, and when we looked back up, we were in the wrong lane, and everyone is mad at us. How do we get back to the place we were before? Is it too late to cut across those solid white lines? Listen – it's not as if we're going the opposite direction. We're just on the wrong side of a fork in the road. There are still many valuable attributes in which we excel. I've not forgotten those things. I promise I'll talk about those things if you can grin and bear it through the first few chapters. At first, it might be a bit tough to hear, so I've added some cute drawings of animals throughout the book to help you get through it. You're welcome.

NAMING THE BOOK

My guess is that very few authors choose the title of their book because of the letters' shapes. Typically, it's the meaning. Less commonly, a title might be chosen for how it sounds. Perhaps it rhymes or uses alliteration. For this book, the shape of the letter Y played a large part in the selection process. It's no coincidence that the big Y on the cover of this book looks like a fork in a road. It represents the gore that's now between us and the direction we were once heading. The letter Y is symbolic of the future we will have if we continue the way we're going, and the future we could have if we change lanes.

The Y obviously represents Generation Y as well. Millennials are perceived much differently than in 2005 — we went from being seen as hopeful world-changers to selfish hipsters. For me, the title of this book is an activist statement for us to go back to our 2005 selves (before we were known as Millennials), and take back the description we once had. In this book, I want to remind you that we're the masters of our own fate. So let's get all Ocean's Eleven on our generation and steal back our identity. As Joshua and Caleb said to the Israelites regarding the Promised Land, which was filled with giants, "we can certainly do it" (Numbers 13:30, NIV).

I don't want you to get the impression that Millennials are the only ones facing this problem. Christians have been falling asleep at the wheel and missing their exit for thousands of years. It's only by God's grace that a few believers have been able to change lanes and show the rest of us how it's done. We owe our understanding and Christian freedoms to a handful of radical individuals who acted counter-culturally in their time, pushing us closer to God (think Martin Luther, John Wesley, even Bill Johnson). But why does it have to be that way? Why do only a few individuals make real progress? Why do we so commonly reject the outlier? Can't we all strive to pay attention to God's voice and move forward as one? It's as if we want our relationships with Jesus to be like a train on the same predictable route as those who have come before us. Some young adults at The Point Church who have been through our discipleship programs ask me how to progress even further. They want to know what's next for them. Whenever they ask, I tell them, "The tracks have ended. The train goes no further." At this point, they're typically intrigued but still don't quite understand. Then I say, "Here are some car keys, and there is your car. Steer us." If we want to lead God's people, we need to set the course not just follow a predetermined path. Many of our predecessors got it wrong. They took us on routes that veered away from God's purposes. They were comfortable or tradition-focused. I believe God is looking for a people who will advance his kingdom by embracing the fullness of *his* pattern, not the patterns of denominations and regulations.

I wrote this book because I realized it's time for us, as a generation of believers to look up and not just realize our potential, but actually adjust our path to get us to the destination God has for us. Let's change things while we're on this planet. And not just ourselves as individuals, but the church as an entity. Let's be more genuine and more authentic. Let's be bolder and purer. Let's give more, let's pray more, and let's share Jesus more often. Let's seek God, find him, and change our lives to match what we see. How can we do that? Well, keep reading.

1

GENERATIONAL LANDSCAPE

To understand what Millennials need to do to overcome our hurdles, we must first have an understanding of the generations who have come before us, their unique traits, and the circumstances that made them the way they are. Although the dates are disputed among researchers, I included the most agreed upon breakdown. Here's a brief overview:

THE GREATEST GENERATION:
Born 1900 to 1924

Coined by the journalist and author Tom Brokaw, this name refers to the quality of character inside the people born at this time. Not only did they have to endure the Great Depression, but they are also the ones who fought in World War II and saved the world from the clutches of tyrants. These people were not strangers to hardship, and that hardship forged something great within them. There are not many people from this generation who are still alive, and if you know someone who is, they're likely a great-grandparent.

THE SILENT GENERATION:
Born 1925 to 1945

This group could potentially contain your grandparents. Some members of this generation also fought in World War II. They may have also served in the Korean War. Many of these individuals (perhaps overshadowed by their parents' strength) did their duties and responded to crisis, but they were so young that they became slightly jaded. Time Magazine coined the term "Silent Generation" based on their desire for normalcy amidst their contingent. The McCarthy trials, civil rights riots, and injustices of the time caused this generation to become tired of conflict, and so they remained largely silent later in life.

BABY BOOMERS:
Born 1946 to 1964

After World War II, life began to stabilize and people (high on survival) began to mate. The rapid increase in the birth rate led to the term "baby boom," and this new, large population of young people formed their own voice. Generally, Baby Boomers were seen to be very different from previous generations, rejecting traditional values that had been in place for years. This generation experienced the hippie movement, the Watergate scandal, and the draft. Some fought in the highly contested Vietnam War which brought disillusionment, and others dodged the draft because they disagreed with U.S. involvement. It's safe to say Boomers were more passionate about putting their hands to work in business and in the economy, which led to great prosperity. If you're a Millennial, either your parents or grandparents will fall into this category.

GENERATION X:
Born 1965 to 1981

Also known as Baby Busters and Post-Boomers, the term Generation X was coined by Canadian author, Douglas Coupland, in his book of tales with the same name. With relative stability in the world and a wealthy population, America was more focused inwardly than outwardly during the formative years of this generation. Issues of the day included the AIDS epidemic, the war on drugs, peer pressure, and bullying. Generation X is not overly enthusiastic, but they care very deeply about personal freedoms. In fact, recent studies have shown that despite criticism saying Gen X was over-stimulated and overly aggressive as teens, they are actually very well-rounded in their adult years. If you're a younger Millennial, your parents are likely Gen Xers. If you're an older Millennial, you might have older siblings who are in Gen X.

MILLENNIALS:
Born 1982 to 2000

For years, the name of this generation was disputed. William Strauss and Neil Howe coined the term "Millennial" back in 1987, but it didn't catch on for a long time. They continued to use the name in their 1991 book entitled *Generations* and in their Millennial-focused book, which came out in 2000, called *Millennials Rising*. Throughout the naming process, experts didn't necessarily agree on what best defines our generation. In 1993, *Ad Age* magazine called us Generation Y because we were decidedly different from Generation X. It wasn't until 2012 that *Ad Age* conceded, stating Millennial was a better term.

Reports about Millennials were favorable for some time, praising us for being civic-minded like The Greatest Generation and forward-thinking like Baby Boomers. It's widely accepted that Millennials are optimistic about the future and open-minded even when it comes to controversial topics like same-sex marriage and the legalization of marijuana.

Millennials have been shaped by the advent of the internet,

it's integration into daily life, the rise of global terrorism, and the unique acceptance given to us by our parents and mentors. Obviously, not every parent of a Millennial was loving and kind, but they have certainly instilled a level of confidence in us that previous generations didn't have. The events that shaped our strengths have also shaped our weaknesses – some of which have become very contentious traits. More recently, Millennials have been criticized for being narcissistic, entitled, and unfocused.

GENERATION Z:
Born 2001 to unknown

Very little is known about the generation after us because they are still being born, and the events we encounter today are shaping how they see the world. For that reason, I won't discuss this cohort much at all.

Now that I've finished giving you a brief description of each generation, I need to leave you with an observation. In my experience leading young adults and hearing the criticisms of our predecessors, I've come to realize that children are not just a product of their parents' values; sometimes, they're a reaction to their parents' values. For example, I've witnessed this behavioral anomaly in my friend Adam's personality. Neither of his parents are planners; they're not particularly structured or organized. Nor are they tidy. To make up for a missing characteristic, Adam stepped into those shoes and played that role in his family. He became the planner and the organizer. He didn't learn those things from his parents, but he learned them in spite of his parents. Out of a desire to change and improve society, burgeoning generations will intentionally challenge the status quo in order to leave their mark.

There's one important circumstance in which I see this play out on a broad scale, and I think it's important to note before proceeding with this book because it establishes a foundation for how I view the generational dilemma that Millennials find themselves facing. It stems from the Baby Boomer (and partially Gen X) desire for convenience and contentment. Most of our parents grew up after World War II, which means almost everyone older than them had been through a major traumatic experience together. Yes, some Boomers fought in Korea or Vietnam, but to their parents, those wars were no comparison to the first or second world wars. It's my belief that Boomers (and some Gen Xers) have never felt able to live up to the standards of their parents. In those days, parents were harder on their children. Our folks, in turn, reacted to that pressure by raising their children with more encouragement and giving them more freedom to be themselves. You can see the same thing in their work. As Baby Boomers were entering the workplace, there was a surge of technological and mechanical development, which was largely focused around making life easier. Modern appliances that took pressure off of people were normalized, like the vacuum cleaner, the washing machine, and the microwave. These were all developed in this timeframe.

The Butterfly Effect is a theory (and a movie), which argues even the smallest action like the flapping of a butterfly's wings creates a reaction that is felt across the world. I think this principle can be applied to the Baby Boomer generation. Being so great in number and having such a strong reaction to the establishment, they created a knock-on effect that impacts our generation tremendously. There's a video entitled "Millennials: We Suck and We're Sorry" that sarcastically describes the Millennial perspective on how we were negatively affected by our parents. Hop on YouTube and search the title. It's pretty funny and worth a watch.

To ease their consciences and the stress on their shoulders, our parents' generation (whether Boomer or Gen X) created a world for their children – or possibly for themselves – that is much faster, easier, and more comfortable than ever. This excess of comfort, acceptance, and confidence has defined us in our coming of age, and is now proving to be a great challenge in our adult life. We will discuss this further throughout the book and talk about how we, as a generation, can compensate for our shortcomings rather than react to the things we don't like in the established world around us.

In other cultures and other times, there was not this transition window of child to teenager, young adult to full grown adult.
It was child then adult.

– Mike Dugan

Pastor at The Point, father of four Millennials

2

FREDERICK SANDWICH

My grandfather was a man of many talents. I don't know the official requirements for being a jack-of-all-trades or a renaissance man, but I'm sure he came close. His name was Frederick, and he was a business executive, chef, youth group leader, and craftsman. He liked working with wood, and he would frequently make wooden plaques and signs for his friends and family in his spare time. He had an eye for it, and it gave him great joy. Whenever I would visit my grandparents' house as a child, I would see his work around the house. There was one plaque he made that always stuck out to me. It sat on the ledge above the staircase to the basement. On it was a bible verse from the old King James Version. It read, "As for me and my house, we will serve the Lord - Joshua 24:15."

Just as the verse was etched into the grain, so will this verse remain in my mind for as long as I live. It's a powerful verse, and whenever I read it, I'm reminded of the responsibility that one generation has to the next. Parents have the responsibility of protecting and providing for their children, but there's more to it than that. There's an element of training and teaching by example that is often missed by parents.

> "Train up a child in the way he should go."
> Proverbs 22:6, ESV

Since every generation is tasked with training the next, each generation must come to a decision point, where they decide to serve the purposes of God and continue the legacy of faith. Here's the challenging part: it's hard to pass anything on if you haven't done anything. It's hard to leave an inheritance if you haven't saved anything. I'm not sure if my grandfather understood the full, generational implications of these words when he made the plaque, but I know he had a genuine revelation of what it meant in his life and for his own children. I respect him for that, and it's one of the reasons my wife and I named our firstborn son Frederick.

Shortly after my son Frederick was born, my father wrote an article on his blog entitled, "The Middle." When he wrote the article, my other grandfather, Walter (I called him Poppa and will refer to him this way from now on for clarity), was suffering from Alzheimer's Disease. My poppa was confused much of the time, and he needed a lot of care. "The Middle" outlined my role and my dad's role as caretakers for generations on the edge of life. To my left, I had a newborn baby who needed my attention and to my dad's right, an 80 year-old man who needed the same level of care as the newborn. We were there, in the middle, caring for the men on the peripherals. For me, reading his article solidified the notion of generational dependence – not as a bad thing, but as something intentionally designed by the Lord.

I want to be clear. My point is not that generation A owes something to generation B. No, my point is that every believer owes something to their history and to their future. It's not a question of this generation versus that generation; it's not even a question of biological family. This is a spiritual principle. No man is an island. In every area of life, you will be blessed when you honor those who have gone before you by taking their words to heart, and by training those behind you to do their part.

If I'm going to give a baton to somebody, who do I want to invest into? I'd look and I would make sure I see somebody who I can build into.

– Dave Roberts

Pastor from Wales, father in the faith

3

PROOF IN
THE PUDDING

Between 2008 and 2013, Detroit was undoubtedly one of the most feared cities in America. After the recession, its population was decreasing, jobs were leaving, services were dwindling, and the city itself went through bankruptcy. In 2012, the murder rate hit a 19-year high; it was ten times the national average. Urban blight plagued the city. The perception of Detroit across the nation was not good, but inside the city – or at least throughout the suburban area – things weren't as bad as they seemed. Whenever I talked to coworkers or friends from the east side of the state (I live on the west side), they would reaffirm their love for the city of Detroit. They would tell me how things are picking up. There were bright spots where young people were gathering, and there was a renaissance taking place. Everything I had heard about Detroit during that time was negative, but under the surface, good things were happening.

I think Detroiters became victims to the label that was put on them. Was it warranted? Absolutely from an economic perspective, but it painted the entire city with a broad brush and didn't allow us to see the whole picture. For quite some time, I was painting Detroit in the same way. The unfortunate labeling of Detroit is a good analogy for how the Millennial generation has been depicted in the past decade. A few shortcomings across-the-board have hijacked the conversation about our generation, but there is something hopeful and strong beneath that top layer. In the next few chapters, we'll deal with that ugly top layer, so that later in the book, we can find the gold beneath it.

For Millennials who want to shed this reputation, it's going to be a challenge. In my opinion, rewriting established stereotypes can be difficult because it requires a track record. If our generation is more than the collection of complaints made by our employers and our parents, then it's on us to prove it. I once counseled a young couple who wanted to get married. They had matured exponentially in the months leading up to our meeting, and I recognized their growth. But most other people had not; they saw them as young, reckless, and naïve. The vast majority of people in our church didn't approve of the relationship or at least didn't think they were ready to get married. I told them that it wasn't enough to have matured, but they had to show people they had matured. At first, they didn't think it was fair to have to change their image when they had already changed their hearts, but the Bible says, "People look at the outward appearance, but the LORD looks at the heart." (1 Samuel 16:7, NIV). I was taught early that this verse is not discounting the need for keeping up appearances. The fact that man looks at the outward appearance should encourage us to pursue an accurate representation on the outside that displays who we are on the inside.

It's not enough to simply be dissatisfied about misrepresentation. Expressing disagreement changes nothing, and complaining about it makes it worse. If you care about our generation's future and our reputation among our predecessors, the only fruitful solution is to slowly change their opinion by changing their experiences with us. It doesn't happen quickly, and it requires diligence. Turning the tide of judgment is a long game, not a short game; it's about the war, not the battle. This kind of effort is hard for us as Millennials, but I think we're motivated enough to change the course of our generation.

On a practical level, changing the tide of our behavior, so the world can recognize our strengths means we have to address some of our very real shortcomings. For our strengths to be seen, we must first deal with our weaknesses and remove them from the equation. Later in the book, I will expand on the high points of the Millennial generation and go beyond the secular understanding of our success to see how our distinctive traits can be used for the kingdom of God. Before we go there, we are obliged – and we owe it to ourselves – to have the conversation about the things that hold us back. It might hurt a bit, but it's going to be worth it. Stick with me. Here's a cute drawing of a bunny to help it go down a little easier:

Have you ever wondered where can we go to discover our weaknesses? Who can tell us what we need to work on? Go no further than your friendly, neighborhood, senior citizen. Perhaps, I wouldn't approach my grandfather for new ideas or fresh thinking, but when I need perspective on life that's bigger than my own, age matters. In Exodus 18, the father-in-law of Moses, Jethro, joined the Israelites and observed how Moses led the people. You would think that Moses, God's chosen leader, would not need input or feedback from a non-Israelite Shepherd – especially not from his in-laws. In this story, Jethro sees Moses dealing with every case brought to him by the Israelites, whether large or small. Perplexed, Jethro approaches Moses and asks him why he uses that method. Can you imagine your significant other's father coming to your house and criticizing your work? Jethro suggests that Moses should implement a system where he could appoint trusted leaders to carry the responsibility for dealing with the smaller issues, so that he could focus on the larger ones. It seems obvious, but sometimes experience sees solutions that zeal does not.

There's something to say for being slapped upside the head every once in awhile. As young adults, we still need to be corrected by our elders and parents sometimes. I'm afraid that we may have lost an element of healthy and necessary feedback in our lives by disregarding (or in some cases, removing) that senior voice of reason. The story of Moses and Jethro teaches us the value of a stern rebuke. The input of a father-in-law figure is symbolic of a rational and experienced perspective. Each of us needs someone to call out our foolishness and speak the truth in love. We need someone to say, "Hey dummy, you're doing it wrong!" Unfortunately, our generation has withdrawn permission for our elders to speak into our lives. That's why it's our responsibility to go back to our parents, grandparents, and the older people in our church to ask them their opinion on how we're doing. It would be healthy for us to submit our ways to them for examination and critique. These fathers and mothers of faith have great insight that could really benefit us. The roads we travel might be different, but we struggle with the same things they did, and we care about the same things they did. Of course, there are generational differences, and people change with age. But we are all human, and we can stand to learn from those with experience. It's your job to ask for it. It's your job to give them permission.

For the past few years, I have been doing just that. I've been approaching men and women that I trust who are 20, 30, or 40 years my senior, and I've been asking them what they see in our generation. Some of the things they told me are things that upset them and bother them, certainly. However, they are not things that are too difficult to change. They've noticed the shortcomings of the Millennial generation, but they also notice our strengths. Throughout this book, I've printed quotes from some of these people. I encourage you to read them and listen not with your ears, but with your spirit. There are common themes in their answers that contributed to the topics addressed in the following chapters. The themes are community, authority, commitment, diligence, humility, and honor. Throughout the next four chapters, I will focus on these themes and identify particular shortcomings that we need to address.

Embrace what God is doing in your life today. It feels good sometimes, and it doesn't feel good at other times. But it's to produce something in you. It's always to prepare you for your future.

– Carol Roberts
Pastor from Wales, mother in the faith

4

TURN ON SILENT

Some people call Millennials the Trophy Generation. They call us that because team sports were a little different in our generation than previous ones. Having experienced the pain of rejection, our parents decided that everyone should get a trophy – even if they didn't win. It happened to me. I remember getting a trophy in city soccer, where the engraving read, "PLYSC 1990 Participant." The league literally congratulated us for just being there, for just showing up. You can argue the merits of doing that, but the result is that many of us now feel special for doing nothing. We've been empowered and told (not just by our parents, but also by society) that we can achieve anything if we simply follow our dreams. They neglected to tell us that everyone has limitations. This open ceiling makes us confident people. We believe in ourselves, that nothing can stop us, and that everything will be just fine. Now that we're growing up, we're facing reality like a slap in the face, and we're realizing we're neither perfect, nor all-powerful. This realization is pretty humbling. It comes as a bit of a shock at first. Some of us haven't realized it yet. If you haven't, I'm sorry to burst your bubble, but you may not be as amazing as you thought you were. Here's a cute drawing of a pony to make it all okay:

Things have changed since we were kids. Our parents aren't quite as congratulatory as they once were. Now, the Baby Boomer generation seems to be quite frustrated with us Millennials. Gen X is annoyed with us too. Many of them say we're cocky, and that we have no regard for experience. Quite honestly, I think they're right. We live our lives loudly in comparison. But we are the way we are because they are the way they are. Having raised us, previous generations shaped the traits in us, which are now under such scrutiny. Regardless of who is responsible for our shortcomings, it is – and will always be – our responsibility to adjust ourselves and transform ourselves into the people God has called us to be. Don't place the blame on anyone else; that's the easy way out. Take it upon yourself to change, and God will honor you for it.

ADDRESSING THE ISSUE

There are two styles in which I could describe how we need to approach overcoming this pride. The polite way to describe it is to present you with the analogy of airplane mode. Whenever I fly and I hear the flight attendant ask the passengers to turn off their electronic devices, I immediately reach for my phone, shoot off a few more text messages, and hesitantly press the round button with the airplane icon. It's called airplane mode, and it allows the phone to continue operating while disconnecting it from the cell phone network. It's a rather arresting action because it turns an ultimate connection device into a basic monitor. I think we, as a generation, need to use our airplane mode more often. I'm not saying we literally need to disconnect our phones (although that's not a bad idea). I'm saying we need to turn ourselves off and listen every once in awhile. We need to stop talking, stop filling our free time with phone time, stop being so confident, and rely more on manual input. We need to ask more questions of our elders and parents. We need to listen intently to their answers, and we need to think about what they say instead of skipping forward without regard.

I told you there were two styles in which I could describe how we should approach dealing with this shortcoming. First, I told you the polite way. Now, here's the other way. Shut up. Seriously – shut up. Stop talking. Stop acting like you know everything. The Bible says, "Humble yourselves" (James 4:10, NIV). The reason it encourages us to humble ourselves is because you don't want to know how it feels to have God humble you. The wise man humbles himself. The wise man shuts up and listens to people who are wiser and more experienced than he is. Sure, there are some people who are older than us yet not necessarily wiser, but I prefer to assume they are. I give all believers who are older than I am the benefit of the doubt by honoring them, hearing what they have to say, and searching their words for nuggets of wisdom that I can apply to my life. It's a healthy habit that I suggest you adopt as well.

For practical tools and tips on how to improve in the area of humility and respect, pick up the workbook that accompanies this book.

If the younger generation doesn't reach out to take what the older generations have, they will be lost forever. They need to come, hear what we've experienced, so they know what God can do.

–Dr. Bob Lemon
Renowned Preacher/Minister

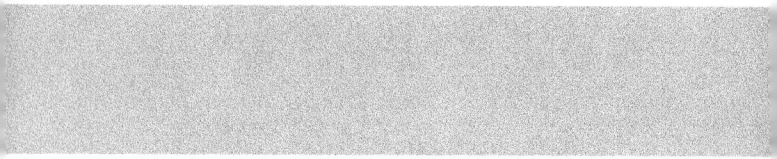

5

BE CHURCH

As a kid, I had different groups of friends from different aspects of my life, like church, school, work, extended family, etc. Looking back, I realized I spent more time with my church friends than most of the others. The church I grew up in had about 250 people, but there were roughly ten core families who had children my age. Our parents would spend time together, so the kids would spend time together. Our families would be at events together, and so we would too. We went on retreats and trips together, and we would even vacation together. I grew up with this sense of community and togetherness that was perhaps unique, but for me, it was totally normal. For our Baby Boomer parents and their Silent Generation parents, this sense of intentional community is not too foreign. Twenty-five years later, having a true church family seems rare. Today, we tend to switch jobs, churches, and friend groups rather quickly.

I'm sure you've heard that our attention span is shorter because of the media we consume, but have you noticed how our short attention span impacts our long-term choices? We become bored easily, but I've also observed our generation struggling to make decisions, commit to them, and to place ourselves in a given environment for an extended period of time.

About five years ago, when I was twenty-seven, I came to the realization that I was no longer a child of the church; I was all grown up. I had become one of those core families that I remembered from my own childhood. It was an abrupt epiphany from which I felt a tremendous weight of responsibility on my shoulders. When you look around at your recently married friends, there's a moment of acknowledging that you are no longer just church friends – you are the church. Here's the truth: if you don't decide to intentionally live in community and in fellowship with other believers, there will be no church. There will simply be a collection of church friends – just people who happen to attend the same functions. If you haven't yet felt that sense of ownership in your community, I challenge you to commit yourself to a group of believers. I challenge you to be the church instead of go to church.

Blaming our parents or our society for our non-committal tendencies is the obvious course for many, but it only perpetuates the stereotype that our generation isn't trustworthy. Is that something you're okay with? I, for one, am not willing to succumb to the negative assumptions that already exist about me. I think it's time to change. It really is – not for our critics, for us. It's time we take ownership and responsibility for ourselves, but more importantly, for the future of God's church. Instead of reverting to excuses, let's do something about our shortcomings. In church life, specifically, this means we can no longer attend church. We must be it. To help you deal with this harsh truth, here's a cute drawing of a monkey:

How do you see the church? To what would you compare it? In the Word, it's a family of individuals who have been called together with a purpose and for a common vision, but when I look around, I see people who treat church as if it's a concert or a movie theatre. To some people, it's merely something to witness or be entertained by. The phrase "attending church" doesn't even make biblical sense. We are never meant to simply attend a church meeting – we are meant to be the church, which is God's representation on the earth. As the church, we are called to extend the kingdom of God, make disciples for Jesus, care for each other, and be in fellowship together. You can't do all of that on a Sunday morning. It has to be part of our lives.

At The Point Church, we commonly have people visit who come from more traditional denominations. Often, they attend their traditional service on Sunday mornings and join us on a Sunday night or Wednesday night for a more intense worship experience. At first, I thought it was strange, but after some time, I came to peace with the fact some people simply need refreshing, especially if they're in a dry place. I understand that, and I have no issue with these folks. I do take issue with those who rely on refreshment in place of accountability – the ones who have the ability to engage and thrive, but choose to refrain and remain distant from the community of God.

There's another archetype I encounter quite frequently. It's a large contingent of people who attend church for that same personal refreshing, but aren't committed or accountable to any other church. In my opinion, this is an epidemic and a greater danger to the work of God. The notion that you can pick your church based on the quality of worship, the speaker, how they run the Sunday school, or whether they cater to your exact preferences is completely preposterous. Consumer style engagement in church life should not be tolerated. It's ungodly, and it's warping our view of what the church is to the world. Church is not primarily for our benefit; its primary purpose is to advance the kingdom of God while caring for God's people. Thankfully, there are provisions for each of us to be healthy and taken care of within the church, but we must put serving above being served – it's the only way it works. Church is family, and He's the one who places us in that family.

> "But in fact, God has placed the parts in the body, every one of them, just as he wanted them to be." 1 Corinthians 12:18, NIV

I like to use the analogy of a flower. Without water, a flower dies. Yes, a flower needs water for survival, but that doesn't mean it's all it needs. If you are simply attending a church for the sake of refreshment, you'll be refreshed, but you won't notice right away that you need something more. It's only after a period of time (or perhaps during a difficult season) that you realize the need for soil. The soil is the church. It provides safety, accountability, and a richer source of nutrients. A root system grounded in the soil will nourish the flower and protect it from the elements and predators in a way that water cannot. The same is true for each of us, when we're grounded in a local church. Proverbs tells us that, "iron sharpens iron, so one person sharpens another" (Proverbs 27:17, NIV). Think about that for a second. The removal of covenant relationships that encourage discipleship and growth makes you dull. If your only interaction with God's people happens once a week on a Sunday morning through a polished performance, it will not be effective in keeping you safe. That's why our generation needs to make a fundamental shift in this area. There needs to be a turning point, where we decide to own our responsibilities and be church.

Life should never be about yourself, but about those around you, those you love, and those who are in need.

– Cindy Best

Church leader & my amazing mother

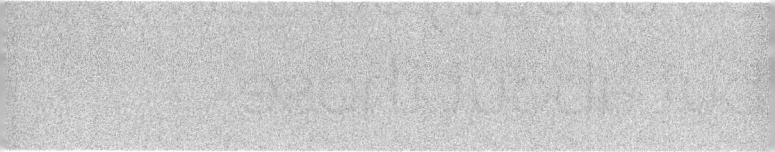

6

STICKING TO IT

As Millennials, our coming of age took place during the age of Facebook, Twitter, and Snapchat. We have become accustomed to instant feedback and immediate affirmation. When I post a photo, I'm shocked when I only have a few likes in the first half hour. Take a second to recall the beginning days of Twitter. Other generations could hardly understand what it was, but the concept of micro-blogging wasn't lost on us. We embraced it. Years later, Snapchat and Periscope added a new element of immediacy and introduced us to impermanent posts. This sense of instant gratification has played a role in molding our generation. These are the tools we use on a daily basis, and at one point, your tools start to define you. I'm not saying we're victims; I'm simply recognizing their impact on our lives. In my experience, Millennials are less patient than previous generations and our attention spans are shorter. It was not uncommon in the 50's, 60's, and 70's to work for one company your entire life. We, on the other hand, become bored more quickly. I'm a perfect example. After a year in one job, I start to get itchy feet. Other factors like a changing workforce and the fact we're still young in age may contribute to our non-committal tendencies, but there's also a shortcoming in our character that needs attention. We'd be foolish to deny it and shift all the blame.

Our relationship with the digital world isn't solely responsible for shortening our attention spans. The belief systems of our parents play a part as well. Baby Boomers, in particular, were the first generation in the twentieth century to break the mold. So, in an effort to raise their children differently, they decided to inspire us instead of pressure us. We were told that we could achieve anything we set our minds to (if not by our parents and teachers, than by cultural messages). We were encouraged to reach for the stars. As a result, boredom in a less than perfect job is kind of inevitable. In many cases, I think we suffer not only from short attention spans but also from latent dissatisfaction. When you set your sights on changing the world, it's hard to shovel french fries at McDonald's. Pride in simple work and manual labor have been almost eradicated in our generation.

Unfortunately, diligence and modesty are endangered qualities among Millennials. Before you conclude that these qualities aren't very important consider what the Bible says about them:

"Let us not become weary in doing good, for at the proper time we will reap a harvest if we do not give up." Galatians 6:9, NIV

"Do everything without complaining and arguing, so that no one can criticize you. Live clean, innocent lives as children of God, shining like bright lights in a world full of crooked and perverse people." Philippians 2:14-15, NLT

"Blessed is the one who perseveres under trial because, having stood the test, that person will receive the crown of life that the Lord has promised to those who love him." James 1:12, NIV

If we want to serve God in our generation (as David did according to Acts 13:36), advance his kingdom, and receive the baton from our parents' generation, we must first be trusted. Trust is something that is earned, which means we need to learn how to follow through. We must be people who keep our word. We must be people who do not quit at the first sign of difficulty. Think about the major decisions you've made in your life and the commitments you've made to the people around you. Have you followed through or do you consistently flake out? If you've held more than one job for less than one year, you've probably got some work to do. If you've ever told someone you would show up and you didn't, you've got work to do. If you've ever dropped out of a college course or program part of the way through, you've got work to do. If you've ever failed to show up when you were scheduled to serve at church, you've got work to do. If you've ever clicked attend on the Facebook event and you didn't, even you have work to do in this area of life, and so do I. The bottom line is that we all have work to do. If you're a Millennial, chances are you don't value commitment as highly as your parents do. Don't even get me started on your grandparents. If they knew how often we quit, they would probably have a stroke. Paul Taylor and The Pew Research Center write in *The Next America* that 60% of twenty somethings were married in 1960, but only 20% were married at the time they published the book in 2014. Commitment just isn't as easy for us, as it was for them.

ADDRESSING THE ISSUE

The first step in fixing this weakness is identifying it. Awareness is half the battle. Now that we have highlighted this particular shortcoming, we can discuss what to do about it. That is to say, we must do something about it. It's no good if we feel bad and don't change. You can't beat yourself up to the point where change seems impossible, but you also cannot wish the problem away. Actionable change must take place. That's why I'm being blunt. I'm not trying to hurt you, but I want you to know that we are seriously falling short. The average Millennial has a massive gap in their convictions in regard to being steadfast. We're missing the mark, so if my harsh words are able to jolt you into reality and provide the understanding needed for true conviction, so be it. I can live with that. Here's a cute drawing of a raccoon to help you feel better:

Thankfully, we don't have to change who we are to change our behavior. Our generation has some unique strengths, and we should not forsake them for the sake of change. We can't throw the baby out with the bathwater. What good would it be to exchange our weaknesses for the strengths of our forefathers if it also means exchanging our strengths for their weaknesses? "What good will it be for someone to gain the whole world, yet forfeit their soul?" (Matthew 16:26, NIV)

Perseverance, diligence and commitment don't have to look the same in our generation as they did in the last. Our energy and creativity are part of who we are. That's why the solution for becoming more responsible isn't changing our nature. You've heard the phrase, "You can take an animal out of the wild, but you can't take the wild out of an animal." I don't think Millennials can be fixed because I don't think we're broken. Instead, we just need to veer back on course. We are the way we are because of things that shaped us. Our success relies solely on our ability to understand and utilize our strengths rather than punish ourselves for not being like our predecessors. It's my prayer that you're able to find the right balance between cherishing your strengths and improving your weaknesses.

Once we have an awareness of the issues and a healthy understanding of what to address, we can direct our attention to being more reliable people, following through on our commitments, and sticking to it when times are tough.

For practical tools and tips on how to improve in diligence and reliability, pick up the workbook that accompanies this book.

When you love someone, you'll do anything for them. So when you love Christ, you will do what he asks.

– Eleanor Best
My nanna, a dynamo

7

HOLY DEVOTION

As a child of the 90s, I was an eyewitness to what I call the "Jesus is Cool" movement. If you grew up going to church, I'm sure you remember it too: the cutting edge sound of "Jesus Freak" by DC Talk, the letters WWJD wrapped around your wrist, and that cartoon Jesus with two thumbs up who claimed to be your homeboy. Even back then, positioning Christianity as relevant because it's cool didn't seem plausible to me. Do I think Jesus is cool? Yes, I suppose I do, but it's not his trendiness that draws me to Him. Beyond my own opinion about products and companies that made Christianity cool, I believe the reduction of Christ to a trend has not helped our generation understand the fear of the Lord. There's a similar problem in some churches today. If everyone's faith is resting solely on the presentation of Christ instead of on Christ himself, it won't stay standing when the presentation is removed. The work of some of these Christian organizations have led many people to Christ, and they have a lot to be commended for. But I simply want to draw your attention to one worrisome side-effect of trendy, Christian culture. It and other factors have changed our perspective of God. For better or worse, our understanding of our Heavenly Father is not the same as our parents' or our grandparents'.

> "The fear of the Lord is the beginning of wisdom."
> Psalm 111:10, NIV

If fearing God is the beginning of wisdom, then we can't even begin the journey without it. To mature beyond our shortcomings, it's crucial that our generation obtains wisdom. If we don't fear the Lord, wisdom will pass us by. As long as our worship songs are more focused on us than him, we won't fear him. As long as we read books and magazines that pander to us in place of reading God's Word, we won't fear him. If the main reason we're Christians is because Jesus is cool, we won't fear him. For us to grow up and truly advance the kingdom of God on this planet, we must learn to fear the Lord.

One of the signs that our generation struggles to fear God is our poor understanding of the importance of purity. It seems that we, as a generation, are bending to cultural and worldly standards more quickly than previous generations. It surprises me how quickly my Christian friends have surrendered their foundation in exchange for the current Zeitgeist. The spirit of the age has been given a foothold in the minds of many Christian Millennials, and it breaks my heart. When you hear believers argue that homosexuality, pornography, marijuana, and sex before marriage are acceptable behaviors for Christians, it makes you wonder what's happened. The loss of those convictions is not only cause for mourning, it's cause for anger. And what will it take for us to say enough is enough? How much deterioration of your faith is too much? Now is the time for us to draw a line and allow no more. We must understand the importance of holiness and separation.

It really is a tremendous blessing to be alive today. We get to experience God's grace in the form of the new covenant. In this covenant, which is a better covenant (Hebrews 7:22), we have his law written on our hearts instead of tablets of stone, and the Holy Spirit will never lead us into destruction. He's the same today as he was yesterday; he cannot deny himself. When the Israelites were told not to touch the Ark of the Covenant, there were no exceptions. Those who touched it died. Although many of our decisions are based on a relationship with the Holy

Spirit, there are certain things he will never allow because of his character. The God of the Bible is the same God we talk to and walk with – there is no special version of God for you. There is no exception to his holiness, and He is not subject to your opinion of Him. He is who he is. We need to come to terms with the notion that God is not just our loving father, he is also a consuming fire.

Society tells us that we should be empowered by standing up for ourselves, defending our rights, and following our dreams. None of those sound inherently wrong, but taken to an extreme, they become the selfish outbursts of a self-centered generation. Paul wrote to the Philippian church and said that Jesus, "being in very nature God, did not consider equality with God something to be used to his own advantage; rather, he made himself nothing by taking the very nature of a servant, being made in human likeness" (Philippians 2:6-7, NIV). As a Christian, do you really have rights? Or did you lay them down when you made Jesus the Lord of your life? I can't imagine any of us would be satisfied at the end of our lives if we only exercised our own rights and did what good for ourselves.

Living for something aside from yourself is not easy. It's also not something I suggest you do on a whim. It might surprise some people to learn that when you received Jesus and his sacrifice, this is the true implication of the gift you received. It is perhaps a more difficult option, and in some light, it may even seem unattractive. But this decision is nothing less than choosing life over death. If we accept society's mold, conforming to the pattern of our world, we will not only be dissatisfied with our lives, we will also grieve the Lord and delay the advancement of his kingdom on earth. Remember, God always favors the righteous, and righteousness is not open to debate. The sooner we realize this, the better off it will be for us and generations to come.

ADDRESSING THE ISSUE

Before we start the process of adopting better habits, we must deal with our immediate standing in the eyes of the Lord. If you have replaced righteousness with sin or God's Word with the another voice, you need to ask him to forgive you. You also need to stop doing what you're doing. The definition of sin is not bad stuff, it's anything that misses God's mark. Imagine his will as a target. Sometimes the things we do don't seem inherently bad, but we must understand that God alone sets the standard of righteousness. We often miss the mark. If you need to have a conversation with God about the things in your life that miss the mark, stop reading right now and pray. Nothing – including this book – is more important than clearing the air with your loving Father and having a pure heart before him.

For practical tools and tips on how to improve in the area of purity and devotion, pick up the workbook that accompanies this book.

I think it's often hard to see any difference in our lifestyle and that of unsaved people.
I look at my life and hope people see the Lord in me.

– Mary Jay

My wise & honorable grandma

8

GOLD DIGGERS

have a confession: I judge books by their cover. I know the famous adage says you shouldn't, and I know it's rather shallow. But I can't help it. My college education and formal training was in advertising and design. I've worked as a brand consultant and a graphic designer, so packaging is very important to me. I'm of the opinion that a good product is worthy of a good package. If a product truly is good, then the creators of that product should invest in its package. After all, it's a simple act of honesty. Throughout my years in the industry, I have come to realize that not everyone who makes a good product is on the same wavelength as I am. They don't necessarily value the exterior as much as the interior. Fair enough. The only problem is I think most people are like me. They judge the inside by how it looks on the outside.

"People look at the outward appearance, but the LORD looks at the heart." 1 Samuel 16:7, NIV

As I mentioned earlier, people see first with their natural eyes, but this verse also tells me that to be more like God—we need to see beyond the exterior. When I look at our generation, I see the same things that our bosses and our grandparents see. We can be lazy, we don't often honor the past, and we're more captivated by digital experiences than real ones. On the other hand, being a Millennial myself, I've seen great things in us that are unique, and I know we're called to a better standard than the one we hold ourselves to.

In Philippians, Paul says he presses on, "to take hold of that for which Christ Jesus took hold of me" (Philippians 3:12). There is a standard and a level for which we are called to reach that we are not currently reaching. For us to get there and lay hold of it, we must be able to look past our shortcomings and see the greatness that is dormant within us. To do that, we need to see with spiritual eyes, not with natural ones. We need to see like God sees; we need to see the heart. This type of seeing is a prophetic exercise. It requires a relationship with the Holy Spirit and an understanding of God's heart. Romans 4:17 (NIV) says that God, "calls into being things that were not." That's what we, and the generations who believe in us, need to do. We need to call out the hope within us until it shines bright enough for the world to see and recognize. We are a great generation, and we have some incredible characteristics. We can't simply address our shortcomings, but we need to double down on our strengths. In the chapters to come, we will examine those unique characteristics that make us special and speak about a future that is brighter than our past. These traits are brimming with the potential for extending the kingdom of God in a manner that is unrivaled.

There's a man named Zacchaeus in the Bible. He was a wealthy tax collector who no one respected. Even the the followers of Jesus thought he was filthy, so when Jesus picked him out of a crowd and called him out of a tree, they questioned it. They didn't know why Jesus chose him and thought he may have been mistaken. But Jesus knew what he was doing. He was looking at the heart – he was looking past the exterior and inward at his potential. I think if Jesus was able to see past the missteps and shortcomings of Zacchaeus, we should be able to look beyond the negative traits of the Millennial generation at what God can do with the positive stuff.

You see those young people up there, really going for Christ? They are the backbone of the church right now.

– Jim Soper
Respected father & grandfather in faith

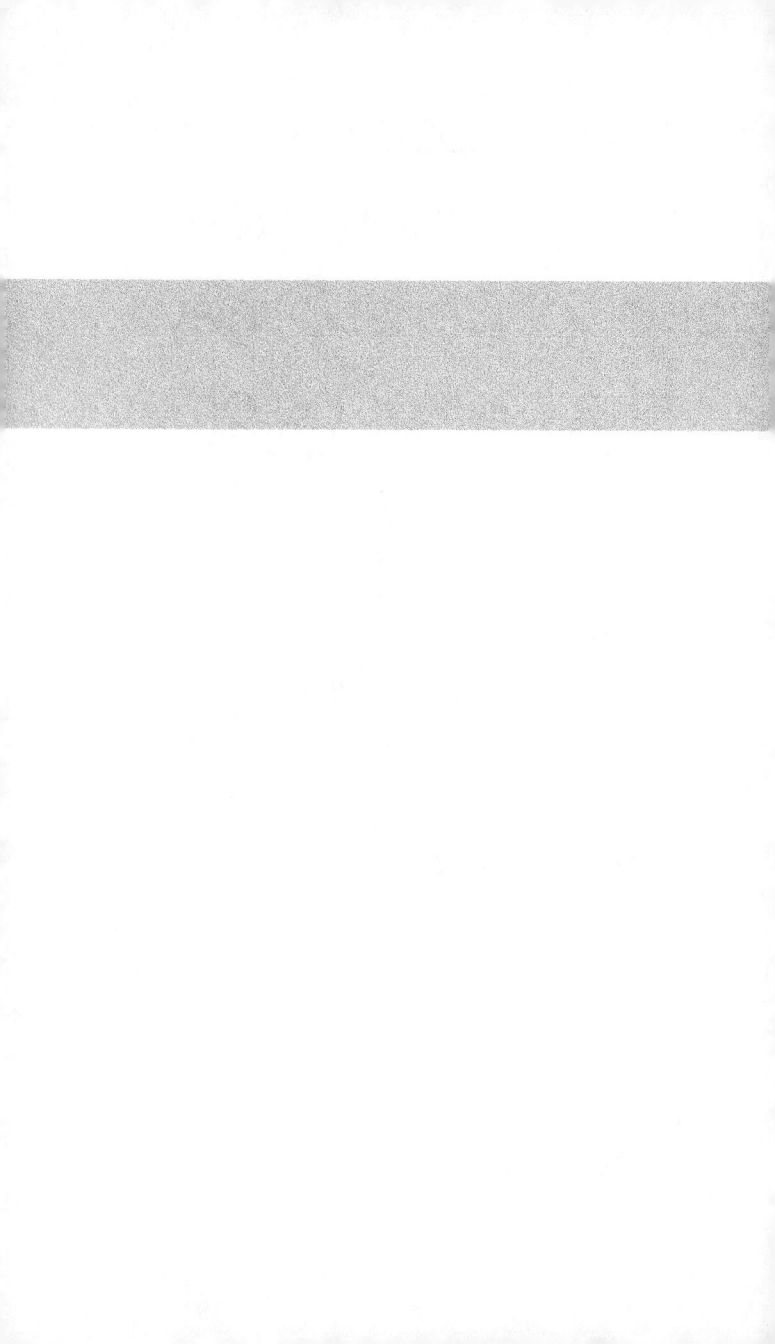

9

UNPRECEDENTED OPTIMISM

Millennials are commonly considered more enthusiastic and optimistic than other generations. Enthusiasm may seem like a youthful quality, but I think ours is characteristic of our generation not just our youth. Our optimistic outlook is a product of our environment not our age.

There are a few events in history that have clearly shaped a generation. For Millennials, the events of 2008 had a collective impact on us. The events that transpired during that pivotal year were a major step in shaping the worldview we now carry. In 2008, Millennials got their first dose of reality as the United States (and the Western world) dove into a deep recession. If, at one time, we were overzealous and dangerously ignorant, it's my opinion that we are not any longer. Years of job loss, bailouts, and decline rounded our corners and kept us grounded. The recession tempered our sense of optimism, but thankfully didn't destroy it. Despite graduating into a terrible job market, and dealing with a crisis we didn't cause, Millennials are still the most optimistic generation about the economy according to *The Washington Post*.

There was another event in 2008 that had a similar finishing effect in shaping our outlook on life, and it had to do with politics. Before I explain, I want to ensure you that I have no political agenda in presenting this theory. I also want to remind you that I'm not talking about individual Millennials but the collective. You may not relate ideologically, but try to hear my point from a generational perspective. Before we talk about politics, here's a cute drawing of a dolphin to get you in a good mood:

In the summer of '08, the passion and empathy of the Millennial cohort was ignited when Barack Obama became the first African-American presidential nominee of a major American political party. His campaign and the slogan, "Yes we can," roused the aspirations and deep desires within a large segment of our peers. It was one of the first times that Western society had seen Millennials rally together and vocalize their collective opinion. Naturally, not every young person supported Barack Obama over John McCain, but, as a whole, Millennials favored Obama by a huge margin (over 2:1).

One of the most popular statements made by the Obama campaign was just one word, "Hope." It was even enshrined on the famous poster of Obama by artist, Shepard Fairey. Obama's strategists had tapped into a key insight about Millennials: we have within us an untenable, yet unshakeable sense of optimism. As children, we were unable to escape the same message instilled in us by our parents, our teachers, and society at large; it was the message that we can change the world. Baby Boomers wanted to change the world, but their parents didn't seem to think it was a good idea, so they weren't empowered by the world around them. Their desire for change often translated into rebellion and guilt. Generation X was certainly a new breed, but the cumulative fear inspired by the Cold War, the aftermath of Vietnam, the rise of HIV/AIDS, and other factors made them realists. When Gen Xers were young (in the 70's and 80's), men and women who lived through the Great Depression and World War II were still in positions of power, so traditional values were still very much ingrained in the social fabric. By the time Millennials came of age, that stronghold of tradition, religion, and conservatism was passing away.

In the book *The Millennials*, Thom and Jess Rainer say that our generation, like Generation X and the Boomer generation, is very much aware of injustice in the world. They continue, saying that, unlike the others, we actually believe we're able to fix it. For us, changing the world is not a dream or a figment of our imagination—it's a viable option. To us, it is truth. The prospect of changing the world for the better was planted in each of us by people in positions of power who had wished they had done more with their lives. We are the first generation in half a century who can actually stand a chance in utilizing the hope within us. I'm not talking about the Obama brand of hope or a political hope by any means – it's Christ, the hope of glory. I'll come back to topic of faith later in the chapter.

The events of 2008 also painted a picture of a highly empathetic generation. Along with our hope that change can happen, our burgeoning generational voice calls for a style of change that's altruistic, often, to obtain equality or justice. Is that desire unique? Not necessarily, but we have the benefit of being more informed about injustices around the world than many before us. New technologies, the accelerated speed that information travels and our social media presence have informed us of the atrocities that happen across the globe sooner and to a greater degree than ever before. In recent years, basic access to information has made the human race more empathetic to the plight of others. In *The Millennials*, the Rainers also claim that we tend seek money, fame or power like everyone else, but for us, it's typically to serve a bigger purpose.

Our optimistic and compassionate sensibilities reflect the internal state of our hearts, but there are also significant and legitimate external factors that contribute to us being the way we are. Before our generation was properly known as the Millennial Generation, we were called by a variety of other names (including Generation Y). I remember once hearing us referred to as Digi-kids. I can see why that one didn't stick because it's a little insulting. But it does convey an aspect of our environment that's very important to mention. Since the dawn of the digital revolution and the introduction of the internet into our daily lives, we have witnessed a gold rush comparable to any in history. The number of digital internet-based companies that came out of Silicon Valley in the past twenty years is staggering. Their sudden and swift rise to power has been incredible to watch. Companies like Google, Facebook, Twitter, PayPal, and so many more have shown us that changing the world is actually possible. Their stories are relatable. When I saw the movie *The Social Network* for the first time, it wasn't just enjoyable; it was inspiring. I walked out of the movie theater thinking, "I can do that." I'm not sure how many other Millennials were thinking the same thing after watching it, but I would be willing to bet it's a higher number than people in other generations. For Millennials, we don't just wish or believe that doors would open for us; they are open for us. The Internet has pried open those doors with a crowbar. It's not a figment of our imagination; it's very real.

Some of the overnight success stories of Silicon Valley in the more recent past further my point. Companies like Airbnb, Über, Lyft, eBay, Kickstarter, and Etsy have provided us with a wealth of opportunity and the ability to bypass the middleman to achieve our dreams. If you don't want to build someone else's taxi cab empire, you can build your own. If you don't want to wait for a publisher to buy your manuscript, you can publish an eBook yourself. If no one in your hometown will buy your artwork, you can go online and find an audience that will. People in positions of power have actually created avenues to make sure your dreams can come true. As a Millennial, you know this already, but you may need reminding that it was not always like this. If you wanted to start something 75 years ago, you would be hard-pressed to find someone to help you do it. In fact, most people were simply encouraged to find a job and stick with it their entire lives.

When our parents told us to pursue our dreams, their solution for doing it was getting a college education. By the time we became old enough to enter our careers, the landscape completely changed. Now, if you're anything like me, you might tell your children to simply start something. In the past ten years, doors have swung wide open that were previously locked tight. No wonder we're an optimistic bunch of people. No wonder we're a little overconfident. It's no wonder we are nauseatingly zealous in the eyes of our predecessors.

APPLICATION OF STRENGTH

As we challenge ourselves to improve in certain areas of weakness, we must also remember to apply our strengths. Being optimistic and empathetic is useless if we don't do something with it. We need a plan to streamline and utilize the great traits we have and not get frustrated by focusing on the ones we don't have.

Earlier, I likened our optimism to a more biblical term, which was zeal. For us to move forward and utilize the strength God has given us in this area, I believe we need to transform our zeal into faith. The difference between zeal and faith is the recognition of obstacles. Zeal is fervor and enthusiasm for an endeavor. Faith is fervor and enthusiasm for an endeavor despite obstacles. Faith is informed, not inflamed. It's not just aware of the positive, but also of the negative. Faith is not based on emotion or principle; it's based on belief. Faith knows why something is impossible and acts with boldness regardless of existing circumstances. In the same way the recent recession helped our generation face reality, knowledge of opposition and an understanding of the truth will help us engage our faith.

> "Enthusiasm without knowledge is no good; haste makes mistakes." Proverbs 19:2, NLT

If we can add knowledge to our zeal, it will result in a world-changing, eye-opening, mind-blowing faith. For us to get there, we must do everything in our ability to minimize our ignorance and eliminate our arrogance. That means we have to be informed. We have to see situations, people, and relationships from different angles, and we have to be open-minded. Add knowledge to your zeal. Add understanding to your optimism. Learn about God and learn about the world. If you do this, you'll preserve your optimistic sensibilities, and you will be unstoppable.

Don't allow too much time to go by before you get answers to your questions. Get those answered, take your direction, and act accordingly.

– Mike Dugan
Pastor at The Point Rockford, father of four Millennials

10

CREATIVE ENTREPRENEURS

n the 18th and 19th centuries, inventors did a lot of the innovative thinking. They were quintessential, mechanical tinkers who envisioned new creations. Looking back, it seems as if only the inventor was granted societal permission to think outside the box. Needless to say, we've come a long way since then. We have been raised in an environment of Montessori schools, start-up incubators, and abstract art. As individuals in this day and age, we are no longer bound to think in the prescribed way we once were. As the first generation to be totally free from old patterns of thinking, it's fitting for our personalities to differ from those of our parents and grandparents. Today's business environment has taught us that free thinking is not only acceptable, it's also rewarded. In our economy, creativity can be easily spotted and supported. Today's Western world is innovation friendly, but only the Millennial generation was born into the fullness of this period of innovative freedom. In almost every industry and facet of life, there is evidence of a surge in fresh and creative thinking. Technologically speaking, it would be foolish to overlook the events that preceded our current creative landscape. So let's take a short walk through the developments of the past century.

IN TECHNOLOGY

Before she passed away, my great grandmother, Muriel recounted her first time seeing an automobile. I remember her telling me the story. She said she could hear it a mile away, and she thought it was a monster. That was over 100 years ago, and the speed of innovation has increased significantly since then. In the 1940s, we benefited from the need to innovate during World War II and an influx of women into the workforce. After the war, factories were booming and new appliances were rolling off the assembly line at an incredible pace. Vacuum cleaners and televisions became mainstays in every household. Consumer airline travel became accessible for the average citizen. Not long after that, computers began to stake their claim in the nuclear family home as Silicon Valley became the technological hub of the world. Today, we carry telephones in our pockets that can access any piece of information we need, and they can store every bit of entertainment we could want. The human race has been innovating and advancing throughout the course of our entire existence, but the pace at which we've done so in recent history is unique.

IN EDUCATION

In American education, we've adopted Montessori schools, charter programs, and online training. After earning degrees to please our parents, we don't believe in college the same way our parents did. In fact, the college system is routinely criticized today for being archaic in nature. In our parents generation, a college degree was a guarantee and a promise. Having one meant that you could provide for a family and live comfortably in the middle class. Today? It's simply not true. The disappointment that some Millennials have felt in their college experience (from debt and degrees that don't lead to jobs) has left them feeling as if society broke its promise. That's why people are stretching out and trying new things in education. My son goes to a school called Innocademy, and their name is a case in point that people are looking for new approaches to teaching. It's my hypothesis that our lack of confidence in the old system is going to propel our ingenuity, causing innovation to accelerate even faster than ever before.

IN ART

Often the art scene acts as the barometer of a freethinking society, and it can a provide an important gauge on cultural progress. By looking through any art history book, you will notice that the increments of time between important art movements has decreased significantly in the last two centuries. Prominent periods in art history like The Renaissance (1400-1550 A.D.) and The Baroque Period (1600-1750 A.D.) often took place many years apart, and they often lasted for hundreds of years. But since the 1800s, we have witnessed dozens of new styles and new ways of thinking about art. Most notably, the original art movements that took place within the Avant-garde show us just how far recent generations have come in creative thinking. In just the first few decades of the early 1900s, the Avant-garde sparked over twenty independent art movements like Abstract Expressionism, Dada, and Art Nouveau. It also presented masterpieces to the world that challenge the status quo. Artists like Picasso, Van Gogh, and Dali are still quite new in the grand history of art, but they're no less respected. The greats of the past century are just as great as ever and much more plentiful.

IN CHRISTIANITY

Last but certainly not least, you can observe this acceleration of ideas in the church. After the early church lost many of its defining traits to institutionalization and corruption in Rome, it took over 1000 years to turn the tide. It required heroes of faith like Martin Luther and John Wesley to recover the godly practices, which were once staples of church life. In every century since Luther, we've been restoring revelation to our ranks. Like in other areas of life, we've been witness to an incredible acceleration of openness in the past century. This increase has resulted in many churches looking a lot like the churches we read about in the New Testament. How awesome is that?

It's hard to deny that there's a new wave of development and innovation that has been initiated by creative thinking. These developments in almost every area of life have opened doors for so many of us, and they have provided new opportunities we can take advantage of. The most significant, lucrative, and exciting opportunity is not simply proceeding in what these opportunities afford us, but to apply more and new creative thinking to what's already been accomplished. Every generation can theoretically take advantage of Über and Airbnb. They can compete in Project Greenlight or run a Kickstarter campaign. But we Millennials have the time, tools, energy, and creative optimism to build on what we see and create a snowball effect. I believe that our generation can advance society and the kingdom of God faster than any generation previous to us.

Perhaps we can even do more in the prime of our lives than what was accomplished in the past century. It's up to us. We can allow our lives to be improved, or we can improve the lives of generations to come.

I believe innovation is an exercise that is grounded in biblical truth. We are creative beings who have been endowed with power by our Creator. We were created in the image of God, and it's our prerogative to be like him. The Bible tells us that the power we have is "incomparably great" (Ephesians 1:19, NIV) and that we have access through the Holy Spirit to "God's deep secrets" (1 Corinthians 2:10, NIV). Applying our minds to such a creative endeavor is not simply an active optimism, but it's an act of righteousness and authority. By agreeing with God and taking him at his Word, we actively receive the inheritance he's given to us as his children.

I've tried to judge key Millennial traits – whether good or bad – on the basis of their ability to benefit the kingdom cause. When I view our creative optimism through that same lens, I see it as a great advantage. I truly believe that we can move the needle on the kingdom progress scale by pushing ourselves to excel in this great trait.

The Bible describes two men in the book of Exodus who are not soldiers or priests; they are designers. Their names are Bezalel and Oholiab. Chapters 31 and 35 of the book of Exodus state that God filled these men with the Spirit and with creative skill in many areas (among other things). God didn't just give them talent – he gave them his Spirit, so they would know how and when to apply their talents. The special dose of creativity that Millennials carry was not granted to us accidently. God, in his infinite wisdom, determined the time and place in which we exist (Acts 17:26). We are not only the products of our environment, but we have been given great gifts by our Heavenly Father, and we have been born at a great time. Esther's cousin Mordecai said it best. "And who knows but that you have come to your royal position for such a time as this?" (Esther 4:14, NIV)

A key strength of Millennials is their immediate willingness to risk all for a cause they believe in, to chase things bigger than themselves.

– Jeff Johnson
Leader, missionary & father of 4 adult children

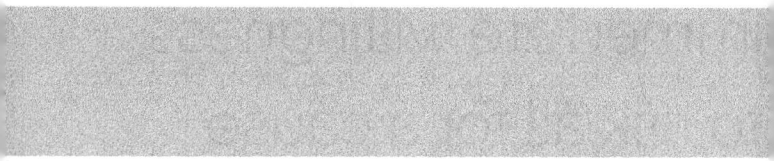

11

CRAVING
AUTHENTICITY

M ost people believe that the human race entered a modern era in the past century. In the last chapter, I discussed the impact of creative thinking on a few different areas of life (technology, education, art, Christianity), so it's no surprise that our collective paradigm is – and has been for some time – aware of our modern age. If, in one's lifetime, one bears witness to world-changing innovations and life-changing inventions, those changes will be felt on a basic level. Our lifestyles are dramatically different than they were even decades ago. These changes are pervasive, and they're hard to ignore. Millennials are the first generation to grow up with many of these advances and new ways of thinking. The Internet was fully accessible before we were fully conscious of its impact.

Personal computing was already part of our culture when we were kids. For us, it wasn't new. It wasn't modern. In *The Next America*, Paul Taylor and The Pew Research Center develop this idea that our lives have been shaped our unique relationship with technology. They identify how we're the first generation who has not had to adapt to computer technology.

I'm near the top of the Millennial age bracket (born '84) and my family was online before I entered high school. My parents weren't early adopters by any stretch, and so I imagine that even a few Gen Xers share this experience with us. It's a phenomenon in which we're yet to feel the full impact of; however, there are some visible reactions to it. Most notably, I would point to the craft trend that's prominent in culture today. Instead of being smitten with the future, many of us are more interested in the slow, authentic approach of the past. It shows that Millennials do not consider themselves to be part of a modern era, in which things are quickly advancing. Instead, we subconsciously understand our current speed of development and change to be par for the course. Unlike many of our predecessors, Millennials have a postmodern approach to life. We actively take advantage of advancements in technology, but we crave the authenticity of human connection. According to a Pew Research study, 77% of high school and middle school teachers in 2012 said the impact of digital technology on our generation has been mostly positive.

The introduction of the word 'hipster' into our cultural vocabulary is a perfect example of our postmodern evolution. The term refers to someone in the Millennial generation who makes their consumer and lifestyle choices with a pressing desire for simplicity and with a sense of cultural irony. Dictionary.com says they are, "trendy, stylish, or progressive in an unconventional way." Hipsterism, I believe, is a reaction to the modern values of the generations who came before us. In a sense, it's a critique of the choices we've made as a society in the past century. Hipsters are teased by some (often for good reason), but the fundamental expression is to be applauded in my opinion. Sure, most hipsters subscribe to a given trend in order to fit in (which partially defeats the point), but the influencers and early adopters of the movement genuinely wanted to be original and found authenticity in old fashioned taste and style. You can criticize hipsters, but there's something to say for finding value in history.

Things were simpler in our grandparents' generation. Food was purer, objects were made by hand, and people were genuinely grateful to have work. With so much focus on progress in the last five or six decades, it's no surprise there's a desire to return to our roots and some of the values we once held. Having been born into an age that is highly developed, Millennials aren't as fixated on the future as previous generations. Instead, there's a nostalgic longing for the authentic lifestyles of a previous time. I see numerous proof points in my own life and in the lives of the people around me.

Here's a list of some tendencies I've noticed in myself that support this theory: I've resisted buying a Keurig coffee maker (I use a french press). Back when everyone else was wearing silver frames, I wanted glasses that looked like the ones Malcolm X wore. I purposely gave my children names that are commonly attached to senior citizens (Frederick and Edith). My wife keeps telling me she wants to get rid of our microwave (for now, we've moved it out of the kitchen). My brother has taken to "old man" hobbies like knitting, fishing, and carving. I prefer to buy Christmas gifts on Etsy instead of at Target because they're handmade and not mass produced. I won't drink domestic beer unless I'm at a hockey game. When I go on vacation, I don't want a souvenir made in China with the name of my destination printed on it; I want something actually from the place I visit. Those are just a few examples from my life, and if you can't relate with mine, I'm sure you can think of some unique ones in your own life.

Our affinity for simpler ways isn't just about new versus old; it's about seeking a more authentic existence. Most of us aren't throwing away technology or even complaining about it much at all. On the contrary, we embrace social media and new technology more than any other generation (see chapter entitled Turn On Silent). The point is – our desire for authentic experiences is more than a preference; it's a craving. You could even say it's a need. But where does it come from? I believe it has roots in our empowered upbringing, it's enhanced by our empathetic tendencies, and it's brought to life by our creative thought process. Let me explain. Most Millennials in the Western world haven't fought in a war or experienced famine, which has afforded us the ability to think creatively. Mix that creativity with empathy (unprecedented optimism) and encouragement (empowered upbringing), and what do you have? A generation who chooses only to pursue that which is truly authentic. What can look like selfishness at times, is really a craving for authenticity. To us, there's no reason to persevere through an endeavor we don't believe in. If our heart isn't in a project or a relationship, we won't pursue it. Some might criticize this trait by saying it lacks an understanding of duty, and I might even agree with you. But it's this need for genuineness that can actually turn dreams into reality. In my opinion, this is the trait that will allow us to change the world. Millennials have the guts to stand up for their beliefs and the boldness to be true to themselves. This is something that should be cultivated.

APPLICATION OF STRENGTH

One of the problems that has plagued the church for millennia is the perpetuation of meaningless rituals. My poppa used to quote a line from Fiddler on the Roof every time we would have a family get together. We would sit at the table, hold hands to pray, and he would sing that famous line, "Tradition!" I loved him dearly, but there's something about that word that bothers me. My poppa valued traditions that were handed down from generation to generation, but I don't appreciate them like he did. Clearly, a blatant disrespect for history is not something to admire, but if you want a Millennial to adhere to a common practice, there must be life in it. That practice must either come from a genuine place or produce something real. If we don't see either the benefit or the heart behind it, we won't bother investing our time, effort, or energy there. It may sound harsh, but I'm just being honest. Could we attempt to understand traditional practices more thoroughly? Of course! But don't throw the baby out with the bathwater. Instead, let's try to find the meaning behind these rituals in church and family life. And if, as we search them, we find them to be lifeless then let's throw them aside and not look back. Thom and Jess Rainer, authors of *The Millennials*, learned in their research that the number of Millennial self-proclaimed Christians is low compared to previous generations, but our passion is much greater. They describe a generation who won't wait around for anyone else to share Jesus for them. The Millennial generation, they explain, sees the gospel as more urgent than ever.

As God's people, his holy nation, and his bride, we have an enormous task in front of us. God has chosen us to take part in his plan for saving the people of this world. We have been given the opportunity, the responsibility, and the privilege of sharing the good news of the gospel with people who are hurting and hungry. If that truly is our assignment, we have no choice but to evaluate the tools at hand and discard those that do not produce life. Why should we perpetuate methods that do not help us achieve the goal that lies before us? In many cases, traditionalism hinders the forward motion of the kingdom of God. Empty rituals of ancient denominations keep us focused on the wrong things. God has given our generation a filter that is pure and has a healthy perspective on both the past and the future. On one hand, we value fresh thinking, and we're able to use the tools that the modern era has brought us. On the other hand, we have an ability to look at the past with an eye for what was good. We can do without the pressure to accept worthless traditions, and without the guilt that comes from leaving them behind.

Since Millennials came of age, discussions about locally sourced goods, handmade products, and environmental responsibility have been reinvigorated. Farming and gardening are on the rise. There's been a resurgence of farmers' markets, craft breweries, and local coffee roasters in developed nations across the world. The rise of the Millennial generation has given society a mandate to be authentic and to bring back good things that have been lost. With this in mind, I urge you – don't discount the ways and means of your father and mother, but hold them with an open hand. Give them a thorough examination. If you find gold, keep it. If you find nothing of value, let it go. It reminds me of what David says in Psalm 139:23-24 (NIV), "Search me, God, and know my heart; test me and know my anxious thoughts. See if there is any offensive way in me, and lead me in the way everlasting." We must be those who search for and remove the things that hinder us.

Similarly, we believers should be looking into God's Word with the same critical eye. For centuries, radical men and women of faith have been finding inconsistencies with church life when they read the Bible. There is a healthy dissatisfaction with the status quo in every radical leader. Heroes of faith have helped churches across the world regain ground and restore long lost truths to God's people. Whether it be owning your own faith, living in the power of water baptism, or discovering life in the Spirit, someone in history took a stand for us to live in the good of these ideals. They fought legalism for the sake of growth.

"You were running such a good race. Who cut in on you to keep you from obeying the truth?" Galatians 5:7, NIV

Legalism is not harmless. You see in this verse that the Galatian church was sidetracked by people who convinced them they needed to follow the old written law after Jesus told them it was now written on their hearts. In fact, Paul asked them in Galatians 3:1 (NIV), "Who has bewitched you?" Legalism can quench the fire of any movement if it's not judged for its life-giving merit. This is something Paul took very seriously. So seriously that in chapter one, he writes, "if we or an angel from heaven should preach a gospel other than the one we preached to you, let them be under God's curse" (Galatians 1:8, NIV).

Authentic church happens when someone sees the real thing and needs to have it. The bride of Christ will never be spotless and ready for the groom if it doesn't demand authenticity. You can be someone who demands it. Be respectful and honor your elders, but you don't need their permission to be the most authentic believer you can be. You don't need permission to be real.

Millennials are noticeably more tolerant of differences than my own generation. This is not only commendable, but fundamental to progressing the gospel of the Kingdom.

– Stephen Best

Pastor of River Run Fellowship & my loving dad

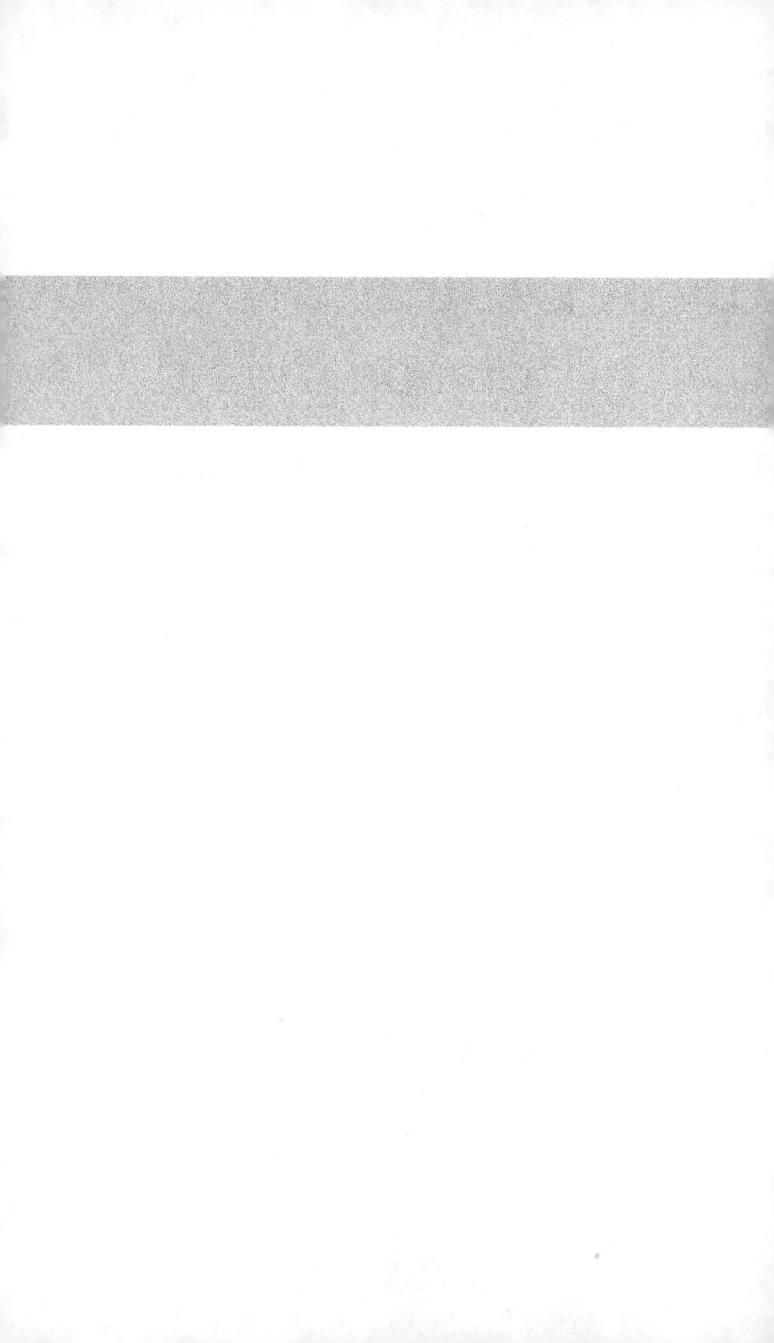

12

THE NEW MILLENNIAL

In this chapter, I will not only summarize our necessary approach for growing up and moving forward, but I will zero in on what the change implies. As Christians, it's right for us to make the shifts I presented to you in the previous chapters (those are the details), and I've talked a lot about doing this to advance God's kingdom purposes on the earth (that's the big picture). But what does it all mean for us? Fight the urge to think that's a selfish question – it's not. It's an important one, so let's remove ourselves from the details and begin to define how a significant shift in our generation would look from the outside. Like a predator circling its prey, let's define what we're doing and fully understand what the goal is. Here, I will discuss three key themes that have been the bedrock of our conversations thus far: self-awareness, self-correction, and confidence in Christ.

SELF-AWARENESS

To accomplish anything positive as a generation, Millennials need to be intentional about their approach to life. No group has changed the world accidentally for the better, so awareness is incredibly important for us moving forward. Our level of self-awareness is one of the greatest contradictions I've encountered. By way of social media, we have become more self-aware than any generation before us. That specific type of self-awareness (which we are well-versed in) is a very superficial type. It's mostly image-based and can be very egotistical. The version of self-awareness that eludes us is the character-based kind. We are good judges of how we look, but not good judges of how we act. Instead of being self-critical about our appearance and reputation, we need to – in the words of Martin Luther King Jr. – consider the content of our character. It's my hope that, in reading this book, you have become more informed about the tendencies associated with our generation. I've tried to provide you with some tools for navigating those strengths and weaknesses, but understanding our collective character is the first step. The book of Proverbs tells us to pursue, "knowledge rather than choice gold" (Proverbs 8:10, NIV). That's why making the effort to inform yourself is a tremendous victory, as it introduces you to the issue. From there, you can choose to learn more or pursue a more active role in implementing change.

If you manage to celebrate and entertain self-awareness in regard to your character, I believe you'll reach a state of fullness more quickly, which will help you become more effective for the kingdom of God. In 2 Peter 3:12 (NIV), the Bible says to, "look forward to the day of God and speed its coming." The prospect of being able to hasten the day of the Lord's coming is reason enough for me to assess myself and make adjustments to my behavior. I trust that seeing the Lord arrive in glory is reason enough for you as well.

SELF-CORRECTION

Once we know what our strengths are, we can pursue them, grow in them, and use them to reach heights previously unfathomable. The same is true for our weaknesses; once we know what they are, we can use the knowledge to affect change. We can take a step back, strategize, and make a game plan for overcoming struggle. It should be a plan that includes accountability from brothers and sisters in Christ, a healthy diet of prayer and meditation on God's Word, and a cultivation of the bondage-breaking power of the Holy Spirit. We have the tools we need to see the plan work. Remember the apostle Peter wrote, "His divine power has given us everything we need for a godly life" (2 Peter 1:3, NIV). In other words, we are fully capable of conquering any weakness or shortcoming that we discover in our lives. Making real and lasting changes in our behavior and attitude means we've graduated from self-awareness to self-correction.

> "Humble yourselves before the Lord, and he will lift you up in honor." James 4:10, NLT

Typically, when I quote this Scripture, I do it to make a point about the importance of humility and how we should put the Lord before ourselves. When encouraging others, I remind them that by putting God first and exercising humility, you will find honor. In this case, I haven't mentioned this verse to focus on the importance of the word "humble," but the word "yourselves." There's a difference between humbling yourself and being humbled by somebody else. In both cases, you've been brought low, but the former is much easier. It's always better to have eyes on yourself, allow the Lord to convict you, and make an adjustment on your own so that God doesn't have to send someone into your life to speak sense into you. If you can give yourself a slap when you need a slap, you'll never be slapped by anyone else. Personally, I would prefer to slap myself.

Self-correction is not only a healthy personal habit, but it also works to remove opposition in your life. For better or worse, there are people around you who are like toll collectors. They stand between you and your desired destination, and they insist you pay what you owe before crossing over into your destiny. If you don't pay your dues, they will block you from entering into what God has for you. Most commonly, these people hold positions of power: they're a boss, a church leader, or a parent. Sometimes, it seems like these folks are out to get you or catch you doing something wrong. They seem more like a troll under the bridge than a friendly clerk manning the tollbooth on the bridge. Some of them are legalistic and change-averse, but many of them are godly pillars of faith who serve as guardians. You may not recognize it in the moment, but these people (who are usually older than you) can actually protect you from falling into error. They guard promotion, position, and permission, but they often guard *your* life as well. Youth can be a dangerous quality.

As Millennials, we can believe that the older people in our lives have overlooked the benefits of diversity, technology, and fun. Although that might be true some of the time, our mothers and fathers in the faith have the benefit of experience. They often know the road we're on and where it leads. We need to acknowledge that. If we don't listen to them and take their wisdom into account, we will certainly meet opposition and, perhaps, our own destruction. I'm not suggesting that we should always do what older generations believe is right. When Paul addressed the children in Ephesus, he said, "Children, obey your parents in the Lord, for this is right" (Ephesians 6:1, NIV). He's addressing the children; he doesn't tell adults to obey their adult parents. In this situation, we're encouraged to honor our parents and heed their advice, not obey them. On the contrary, I believe God has given us Millennials a unique vision for how to reach our own generation. Do we need the support and wisdom of our elders, parents, and mentors? Abso-freakin'-lutely. If you ignore them, you're a fool. It is much better to pursue an endeavor when you have the support of your forefathers. According to Thom and Jess Rainer, our relatively small group of Christian Millennials can revolutionize churches and make a real kingdom difference, but we need wisdom and guidance.

By pursuing correction and seeking wisdom, you will earn the respect of your peers and predecessors. Most older Christians who are pillars of faith do not despise young people. They're not ageist or prejudiced against youth. They understand the perils and difficulties of being young – they've been there! Older Christians are simply looking for young people who have sound judgment. In fact, they probably admire your faith and boldness. What they want is to see that we can receive wisdom, weigh situations, and adjust as necessary. They want to know they've been heard. Honoring older believers is not for their benefit only; it's also for ours. When we ensure that they've been heard and that we have their trust, we can move forward with more confidence and without obstacles.

CONFIDENCE IN CHRIST

For us Millennials, confidence is not usually an issue. Typically, we believe in ourselves and have enough confidence to accomplish the task in front of us. The only problem with our confidence is that it's in ourselves. For us to be a generation that pursues God and advances the kingdom, we must separate our confidence from ourselves. The last two subsections of the chapter were all about "self" (self-awareness, self-correction), but this one needs to be different. We've have a highly-developed confidence muscle, but we can't rely on it. Switch Hitters in baseball are not only strong and skilled, they're able to apply that strength and skill in a different way. They're able to switch the way they swing the bat at a moment's notice. We need to do the same thing now by attributing our confidence not to ourselves, but to Christ Jesus. It's time to switch. He is the one by whom everything is possible. Without his grace and power at work in our lives, each of us would be lost. We would not be successful in our endeavors; we would be floating out on a raft by ourselves, leaning on our own strength. Confidence in Christ is not just a matter of doing the right thing – it's also about choosing the best thing.

"Trust in the Lord with all your heart and lean not on your own understanding; in all your ways submit to him, and he will make your paths straight." Proverbs 3:5-6, NIV

It's easy for us to be proud because we're in the prime of our lives. This is especially true when everyone is telling us how amazing we are and when we're shielded from the consequences of our life choices. Correction is a teacher, but if our confidence is not in Christ, we'll be crushed by our own failures. If we trust in our own abilities, skills, and energy, we will be sorely disappointed when those things fail us. But if we place our confidence in him, not only will we endure trials, but we will go beyond what was ever possible on our own. Your fullness is no match for his fullness.

What would happen if we took the same confidence we have in ourselves and applied it to God's promises? What if we actually believed that we are who God says we are? For the last century, the difficulty has not been doing God's work, but it has been believing God's Word about us. Millennials are perfectly poised to take God at his Word. Historically, simply receiving an inheritance from God has been a radical move, but I believe Millennials are the first generation in a very long time who are gutsy enough to feel comfortable receiving from

God. Imagine what is possible for those who accept the great works that Christ has empowered us to do. As I mentioned before, Paul calls it the, "incomparably great power for us who believe" (Ephesians 1:19, NIV). Jesus said it himself, "Whoever believes in me will do the works I have been doing, and they will do even greater things than these" (John 14:12, NIV). How incredible is that!?! If we're able to be self-aware and if we are able to self-correct, just imagine what our level of confidence in Christ Jesus can produce!

THE MANIFESTO

When I was planning this book, I relished the idea of being able to paint a picture of what I believe God can accomplish through the Millennial Generation. The opportunity to speak prophetically into the destiny of my peers and about our possible exploits excites me. I knew all along that this entire book would lead up to a short manifesto (if you will), that outlines a possible future that is brighter than the path we are currently on. I hope that you can read the following words and allow them to be planted into your heart. It's my sincerest prayer that over the course of the next few days, weeks, months, and years, the Lord will water these words and shine his light on them so that they take deep root in you. The goal is for this to produce maturity; a plant that grows so tall, it surprises you. This is our declaration:

We, the recently young, the Millennial Generation (specifically those of us born between 1982 and the year 2000) – like the sons of Issachar – know our season, and we know what to do.

We will be a grateful generation. We will not be ignorant of our privilege and the circumstances in which we were raised. We are thankful to our parents, grandparents, and great-grandparents for the sacrifices they have made so that we, here in the Western world, may experience peace and provision. We acknowledge that the abundance around us is not the result of our own doing, but the product of the godly lives of our ancestors who were blessed by God. Much of what we have today is an answer to the prayers of our forefathers.

We will work. Although we have access to so much resource we didn't earn, we will not take it for granted. We will aim to be good stewards of these things, and we will work hard to be deemed worthy recipients of these blessings. We know we sometimes act entitled to receive great things, and we know this attitude is wrong. We will work to show other generations and Christ himself that we can be trusted with their gifts.

We will persevere. It's not easy for us to focus on a single task, but we know that blessing comes when we persevere through hard times. We will consider it pure joy when we experience trials of many kinds. We will not give up, and we will not quit until God tells us to stop. We have been flakey in the past, and we're sorry. We will strive to stick to our word, so that our word means something. We want to know the joy that comes from diligence and dedication.

We will join. Despite our inner drive and desire to run and explore, we fully understand that God has designed his church to supply our needs and that the body of Christ is his bride – his plan for the world. On our own, we will never make it. That's why we commit to being part of a church family that sharpens us and holds us accountable. We will also do our best to sharpen other members of that family and hold them accountable to a life of faith.

We will be pure. We will not prescribe to anyone else's definition of what is right and wrong. We will find our standard of holiness in the Word of God and not in the rationalizations of man. We will be separate – in the world and relevant to all—but not of the world. We will look different. No matter how normal it may seem to our peers, we will not compromise under any circumstance.

We will listen. We will shut up. And as young adults, we will seek out the wisdom of believers who have come before us. On wisdom the house is built, so we will put aside our pride and agree to receive the guidance of our predecessors. We may not do everything they say, but we will listen and give their words careful consideration.

We will dare to believe God. Anyone can believe in the existence of God – even demons believe he exists, but we, as a generation, have decided to believe his Word – and more specifically, his Word about us. When he says we are his children, we believe him. When he says that we have an inheritance, we believe him. When he says we have authority to heal the sick, cast out demons, and bring freedom to people, we believe him. Lord, we are not afraid to receive your love and walk in the victory you have given us. We have been raised with confidence, so Father, we believe you.

We will seek him. We will chase him and pursue him. We will be on the front foot instead of the back foot. We want to be on the cutting edge of what God is doing in this world. And when we seek him, we know we will find him. We plan to reach him and know him. We will not forsake spending time with our Father. We understand that to steward our lives responsibly, we need to steward a healthy personal relationship with God.

We will return. We are not so naïve to think that our generation does everything better than previous generations. We know we have a lot to learn from people who have come before us. This is true especially in church life. With the corruption of the church in ancient times, God's people forgot many of the beliefs and practices found in the Bible. We commit ourselves to rediscovering these truths by asking questions and searching the Word of God. In this way, we hope and plan to be an integral part of the great restoration of God's house.

We will break chains. Hebrews tells us that sin can easily entangle us, and many other things can hinder us. We want to see our friends and families set free from sin and the entanglements of lifeless religious traditions. We will not engage in empty rituals for the sake of it. We want to break the chains of religious oppression and tear down detrimental denominational walls, so every person can see Jesus clearly.

We will advance. We refuse to wait and do nothing. God has commissioned us to go and make disciples, and that is exactly what we plan to do. We are his ambassadors, divinely appointed, and called to great work. We believe the work God's empowered us to do will change the world. It will advance his kingdom and his will. It is our goal to see his authority, his love, his justice, and his peace invade every facet of our society. Leaving this planet without moving the needle is not an option for us.

By doing these things and holding fast to them, we will reclaim our destinies and also our reputations. We refuse to be flakey, unreliable, apathetic, selfish people. We want to be remembered for our boldness, our faith, and our ability to take ownership of our futures.

Father, let it be.

If you have a love for the Lord, and you're tenacious, and you're passionate for God, keep pressing. Don't let go. If you let go, it'll never happen.

– Eleanor Best
My nanna, a dynamo

WORKS REFERENCED

1. Abbey-Lambertz, Kate. "Detroit's Staggering Murder And Violent Crime Rate Are 'A Public Health Issue.'" *Huffington Post*, 14 Nov. 2014, http://www.huffingtonpost.com/2014/11/14/detroit-highest-murder-rate-violent-crime_n_6144460.html

2. Rampell, Catherine. "Millennials, America's Optimists?" *Washington Post*, 29 June 2016, https://www.washingtonpost.com/news/rampage/wp/2016/06/29/millennials-americas-economic-optimists/?utm_term=.76ea0c456443

3. Winograd, Morley and Hais, Michael. "President Obama, The Millennial Whisperer" *Los Angeles Times*, 16 Jan. 2017, http://www.latimes.com/opinion/op-ed/la-oe-winograd-hais-obama-the-millennial-president-20170116-story.html

4. Winograd, Morley and Hais, Michael. "It's Official: Millennials Realigned Politics in 2008." *Huffington Post*, 18 Dec. 2008, http://www.huffingtonpost.com/michael-hais-and-morley-winograd/its-official-millennials_b_144357.html

5. Rainer, T. S., & Rainer, J. W. (2011). The millennials: connecting to America's largest generation. Nashville, Tenn: B & H Pub. Group.

6. Taylor, P. (2014). The next America: boomers, millennials, and the looming generational showdown. New York: PublicAffairs.

ABOUT THE AUTHOR

A Canadian living in Michigan, Joshua Best is a church pastor at The Point Church, a freelance art director in the advertising industry, and the founder of Unprecedented Press. He's a catalyst for change in church, family, and business.

Josh and his wife, April, have been leaders of the The Point Exchange, a young adult ministry in Grand Rapids, for over seven years. They are both passionate about seeing their generation pursue God with gusto. They currently serve God in Holland, Michigan and have two young children. Josh has written one other book in two volumes called *40 Shocking Facts for 40 Weeks of Pregnancy.*

E V E R Y O N E

global giving initiative

In pursuit of our mission to help people get their voices and ideas out into the world, we realize that others are concerned with more pressing needs. Finding creativity in every person is important work, but getting food, shelter, and dignity to individuals must come first. That's why Unprecedented Press donates a portion of all book revenue to the Everyone Gobal Giving Initative whose goal is to meet the practical needs of individuals around the world and to share the love of Jesus. To learn more, visit *everyoneglobal.com*

Other titles from

Unprecedented Press

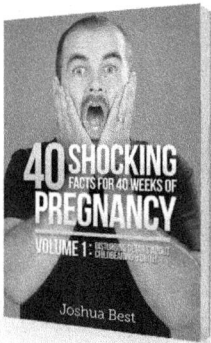

40 Shocking Facts for 40 Weeks
of Pregnancy - Volume 1:
*Disturbing Details about
Childbearing & Birth*

By Joshua Best

40 Shocking Facts for 40 Weeks
of Pregnancy - Volume 2:
*Terrifying Truths about Babies
& Breastfeeding*

By Joshua Best

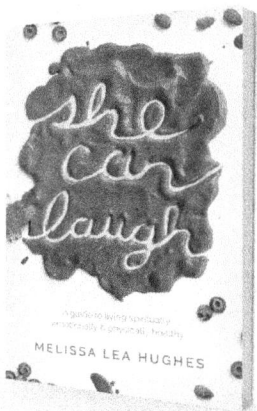

She Can Laugh
*A Guide to Living Spiritually,
Emotionally & Physically Healthy*

By Melissa Lea Hughes

Once Upon A Year
*Experience a year in
the life of Finn*

By Joanna Lenau

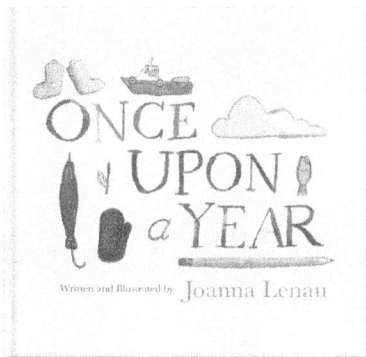

All titles available from Amazon
or from unprecedentedpress.com/shop

www.ingramcontent.com/pod-product-compliance
Lightning Source LLC
Chambersburg PA
CBHW060043030426
42334CB00019B/2466